# German Baroque Music for Mandolin

I0901466

6 Sonatas for Violin
from Hortulus Chelicus (1688)
by Johann Jakob Walther (1650-1717)

by Robert Bancalari



WWW.MELBAY.COM

# *Preface*

There were three virtuosi from the 17th century German school; Biber, Westhoff, and Johann Jakob Walther (1650-1717). Walther was a violinist in the orchestra of Cosimo III (Medici) from 1670-74 and became concertmaster at the court in Dresden.

His compositions are left to us in two books: *Scherzi da Violino solo con il basso continuo* (1676) and *Hortulus Chelicus* (1688).

The collection of sonatas for this book come from his *Hortulus Chelicus.*

*Robert Bancalari*

# Contents

**6 Sonatas for Violin from *Hortulus Chelicus* (1688)**
**Johann Jakob Walther (1650-1717) Transcribed for Mandolin with Tab**

# Sonata 1
## Preludio

Johann Jakob Walther (1650-1717)

Adagio

Presto ♩ = 90

Adagio
Presto
Adagio

# Aria

# Corrente

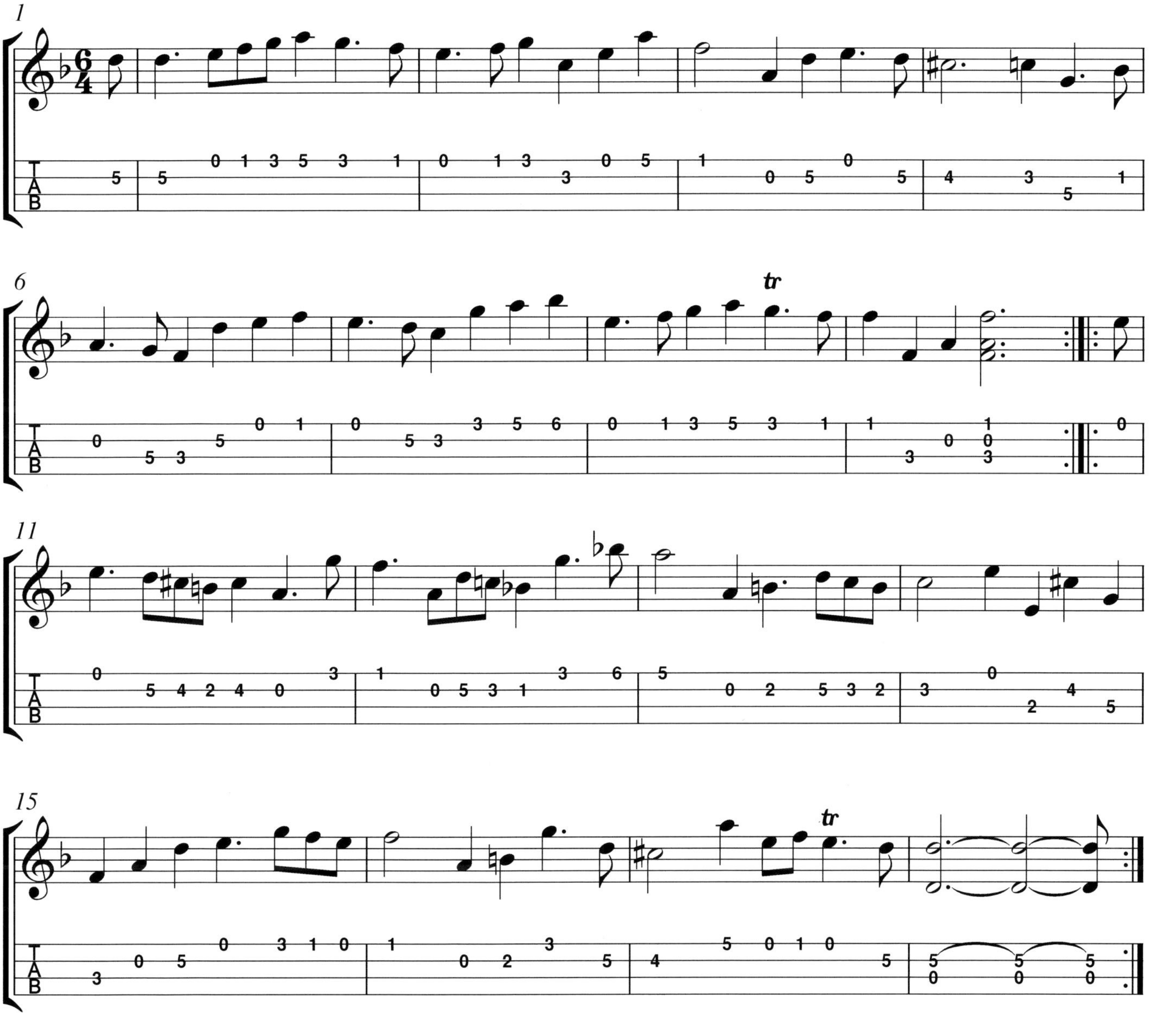

# Sarabanda

# Giga

3

# Finale

# Sonata II

## Preludio

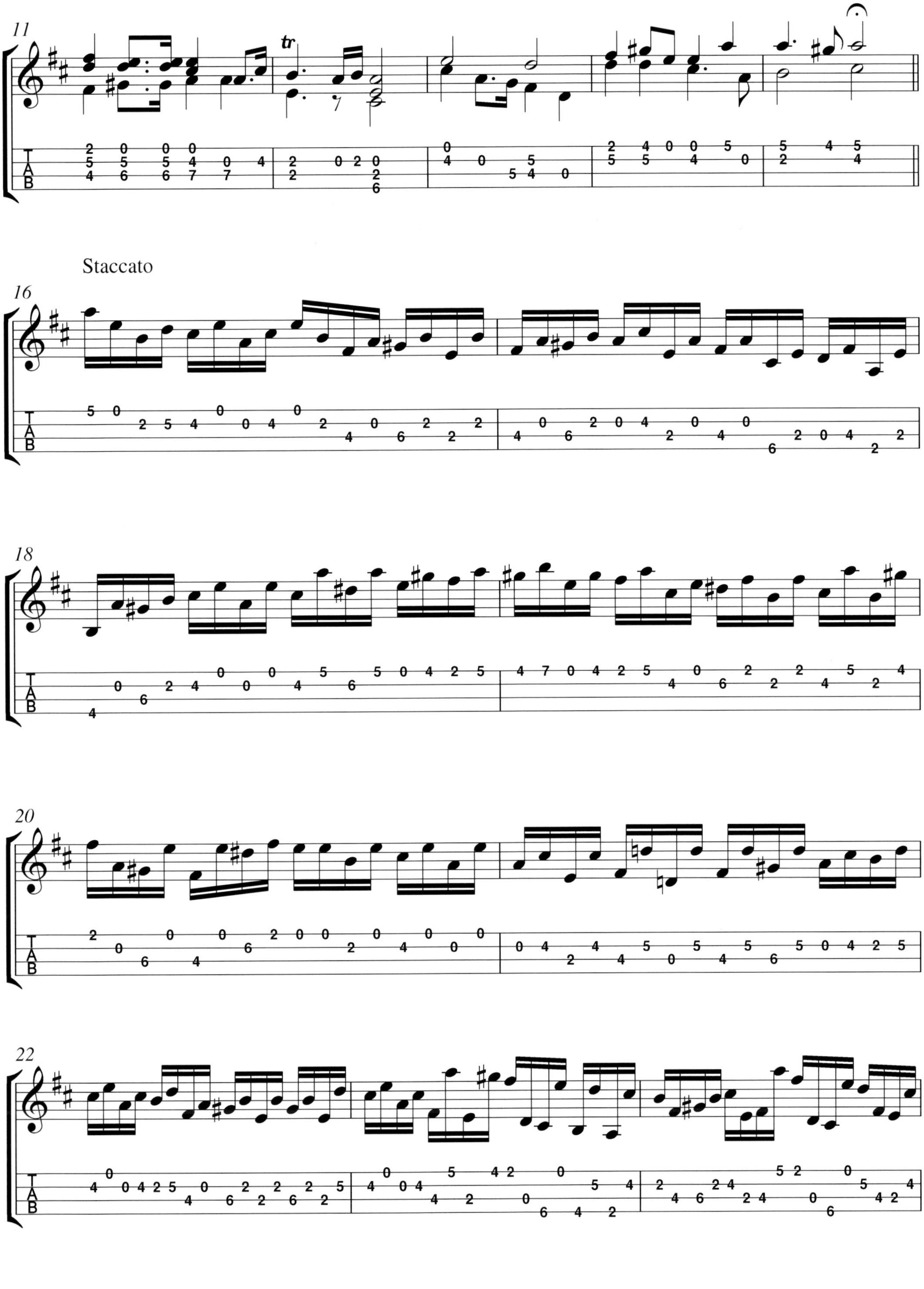
tr
Staccato

25
Adagio
tr
30
34
tr
37
Presto
40
Adagio
44
Presto

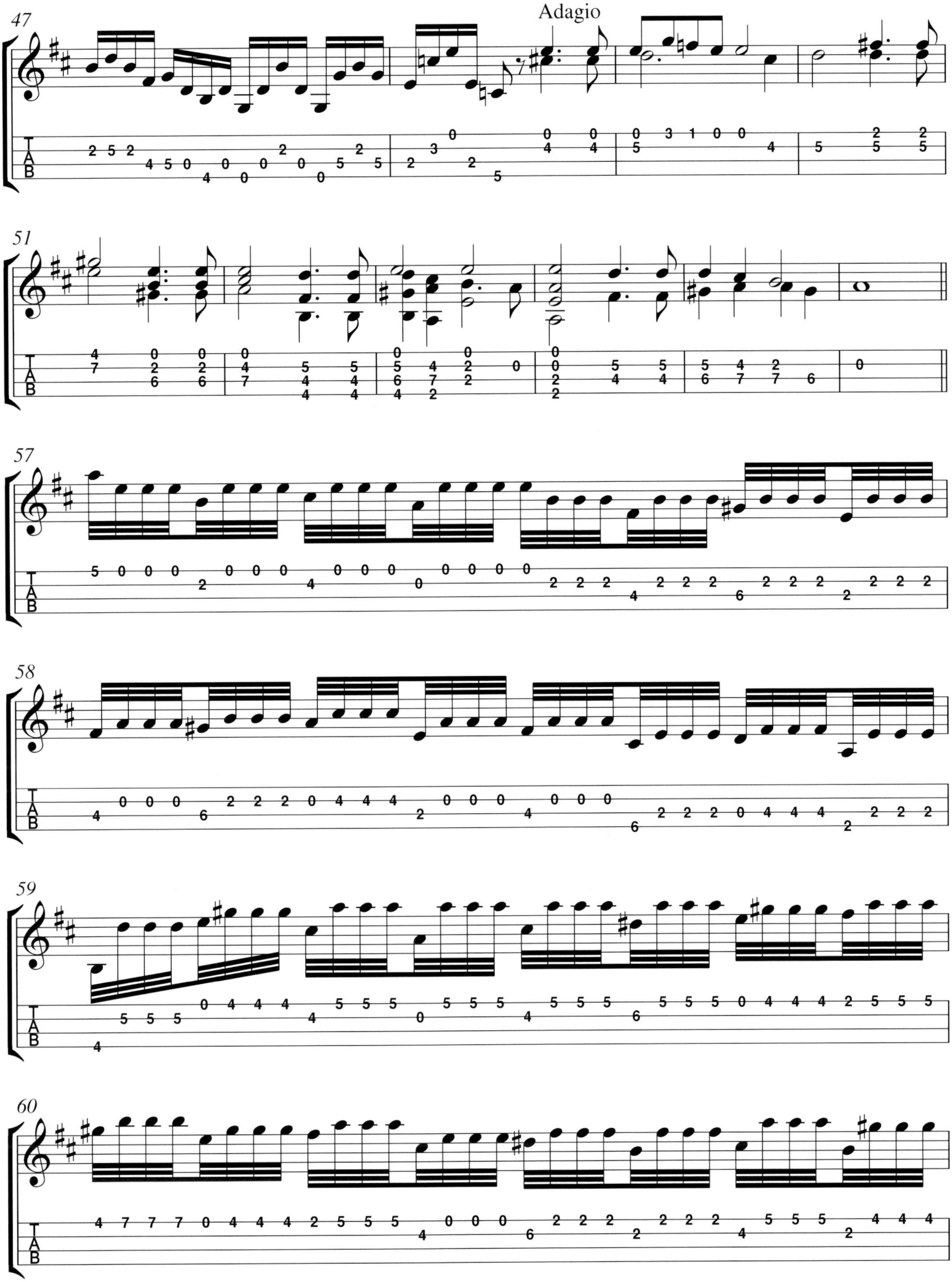
Adagio

61
62
63
64
65
tr

# Allemanda

86
tr
90
95
100
tr
105
110

# Sarabanda

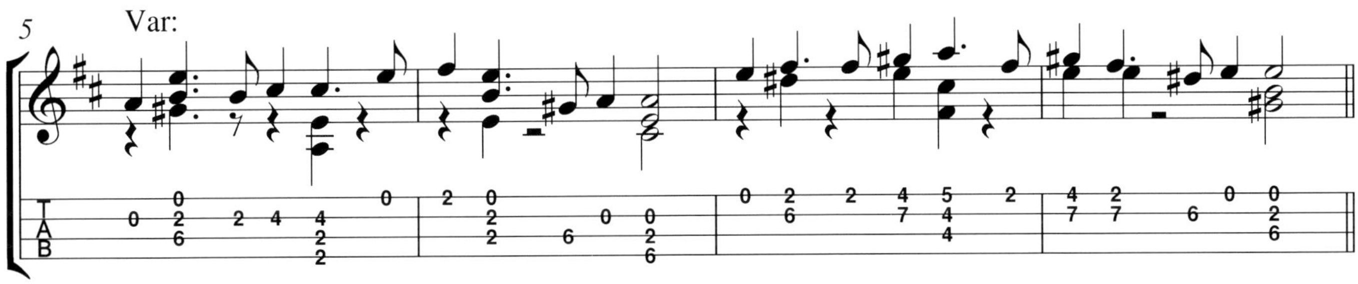

# Giga

# Finale

# Sonata III
## Aria Variata

11
tr
16
tr
20
23
26
29
TAB

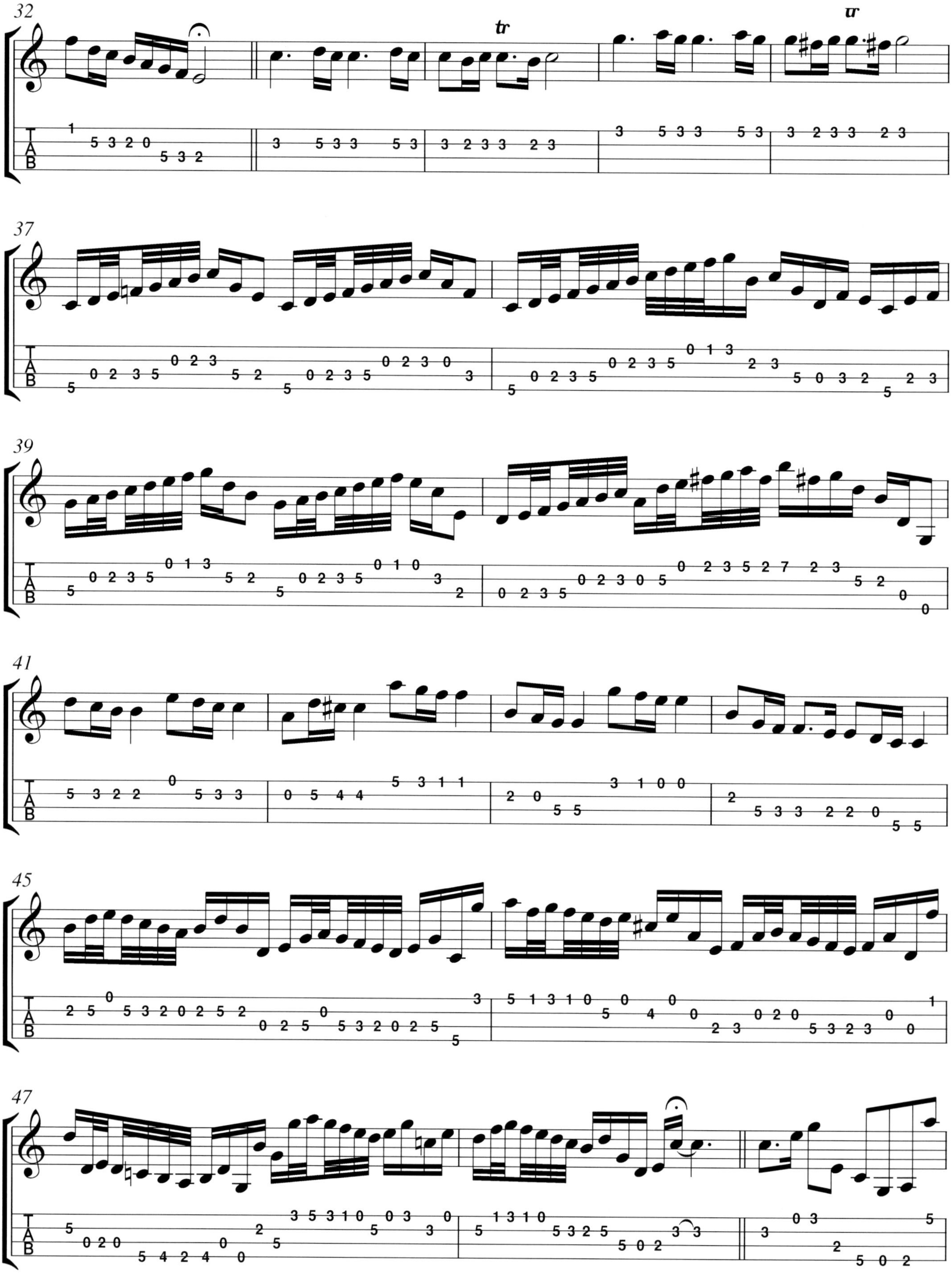
32
tr
tr
37
39
41
45
47

50
TAB
54
TAB
57
TAB
61
TAB
63
TAB
66
TAB

70
72
76
tr
79
82
85

88
91
94
97
101
103

105
tr
109
111
113
12
8
116
119

122
125
128
132
134
136

139
tr
142
144
146
149
151

154
157
159
162
165
167

170
tr
173
175
178
181
183

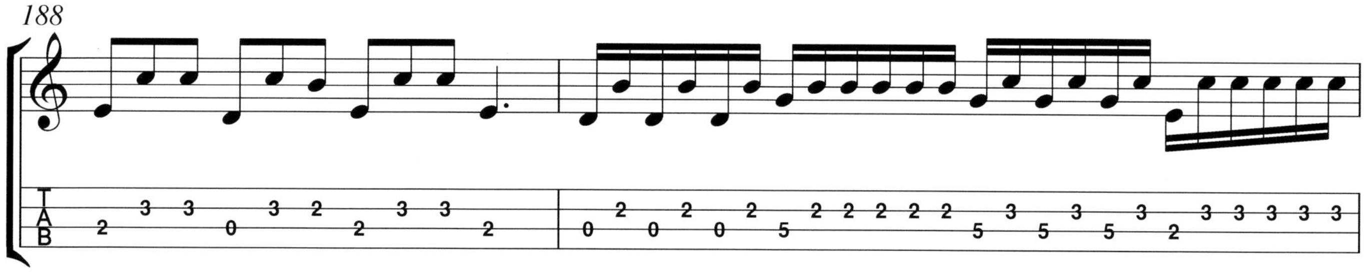


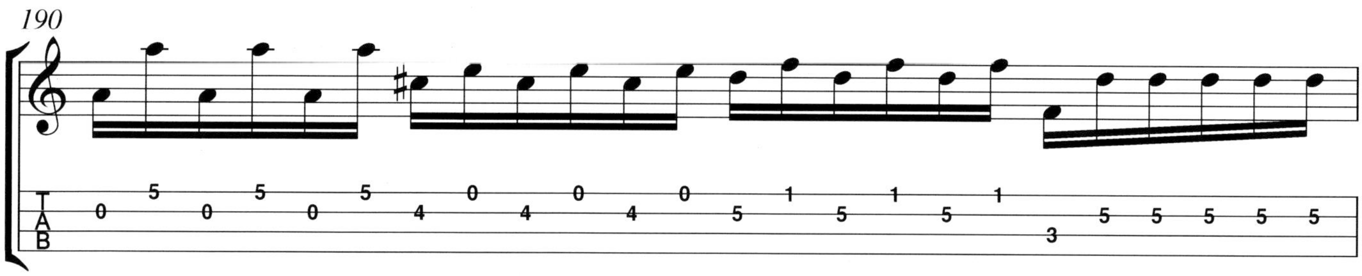

# Sonata IV

## Preludio

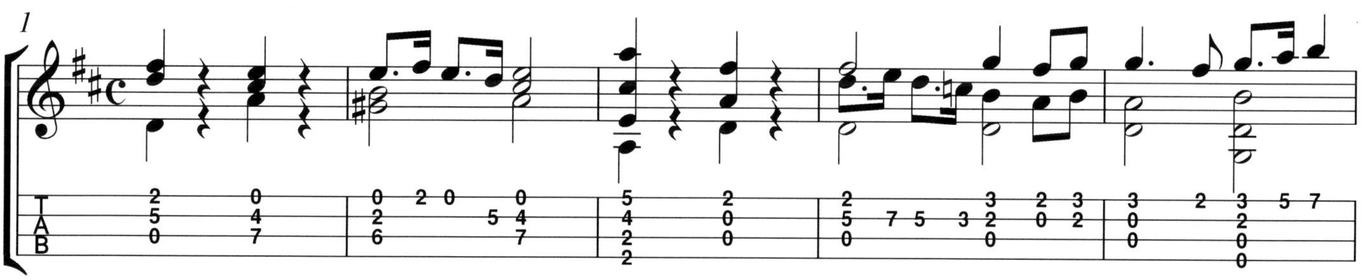

Adagio
Presto

# Allemanda

# Sarabanda

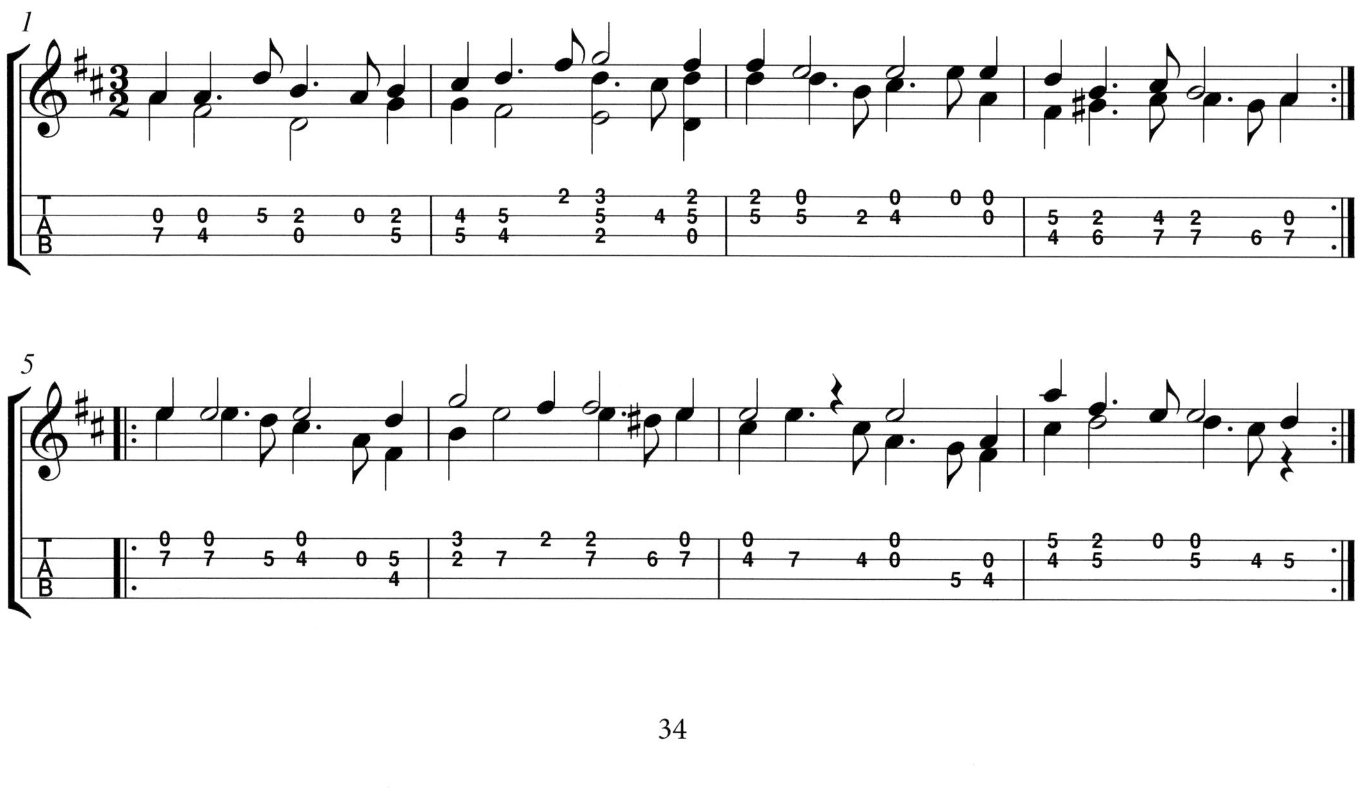

# Giga

# Finale

# Sonata V

## Preludio

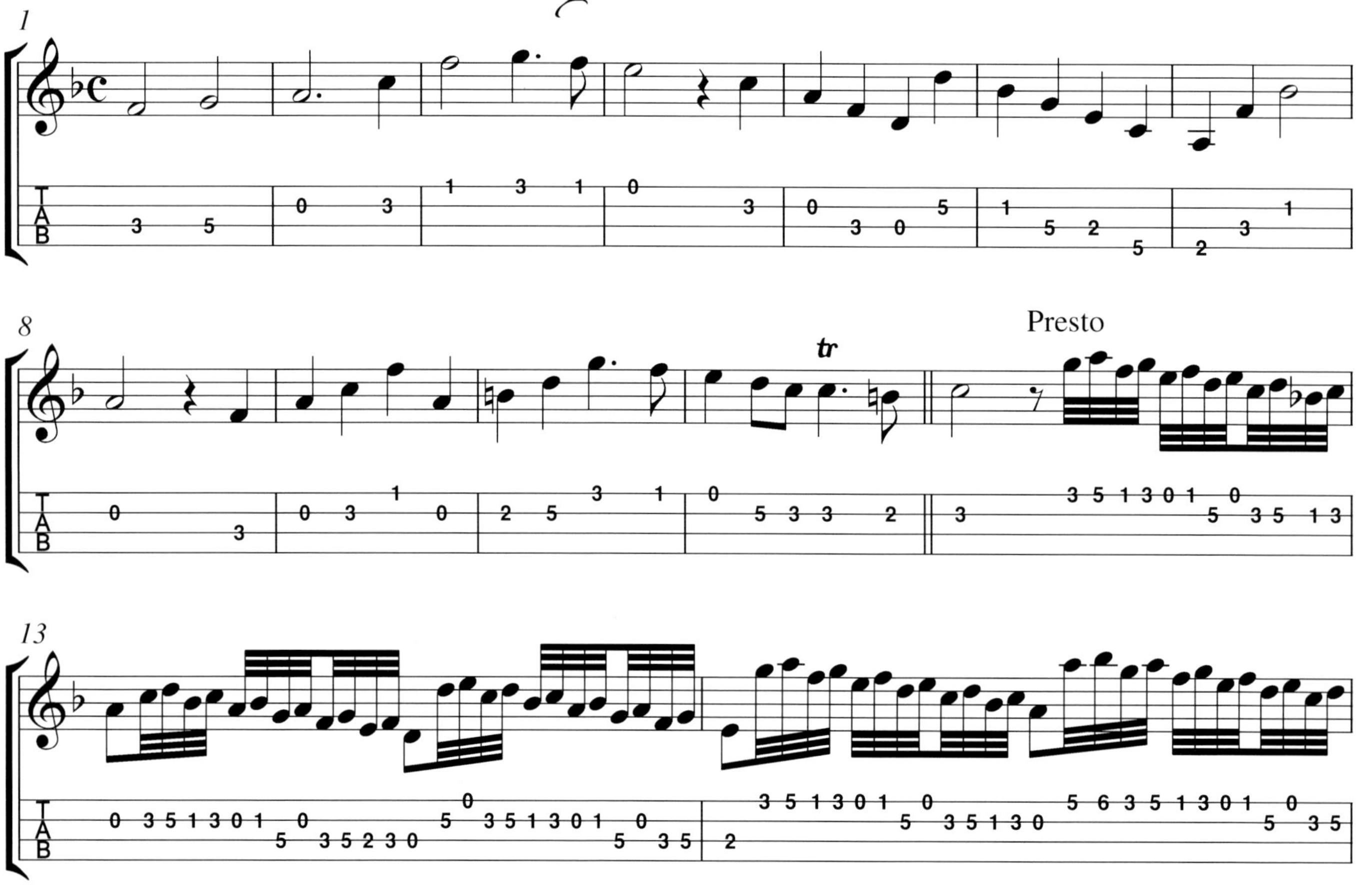

15
Adagio
17
21
Presto
24
Adagio
27
32

# Aria

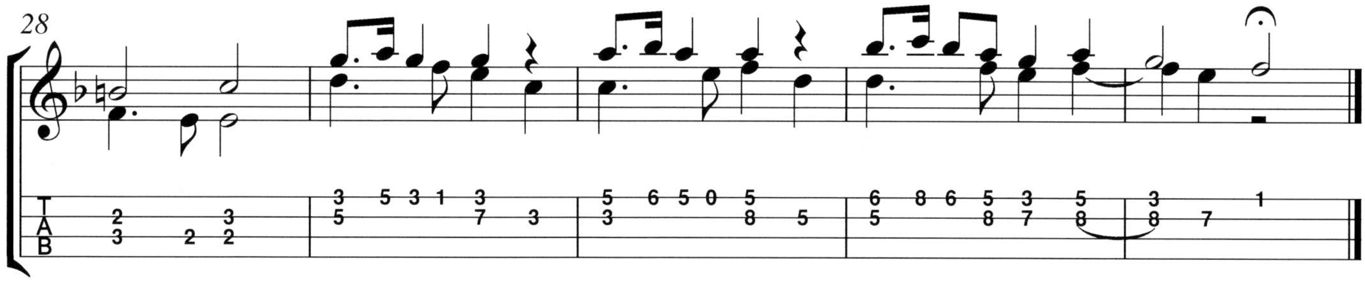

# Sarabanda

13
15
Var:
18
21
Var:
23
25

## Giga

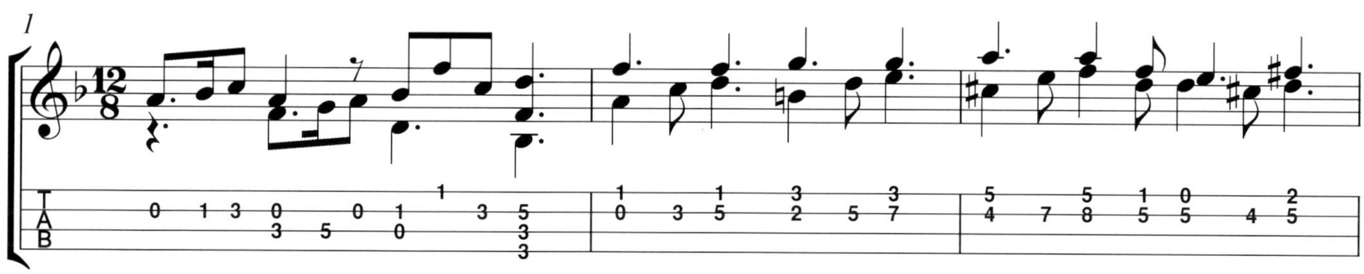

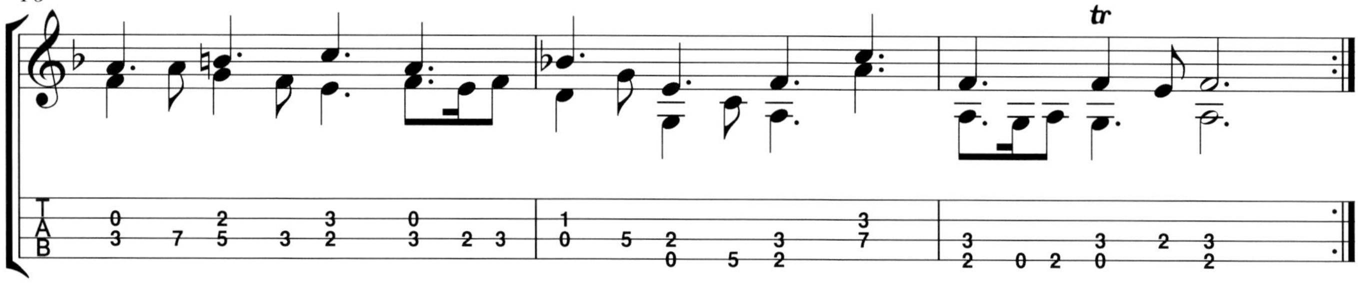


# Finale

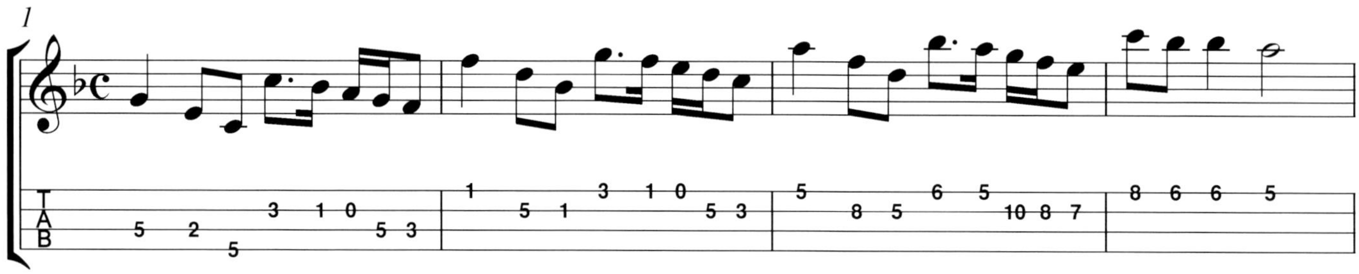


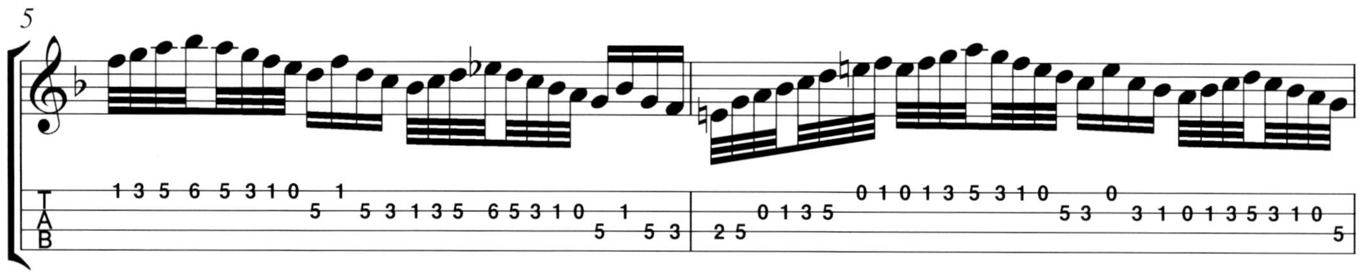


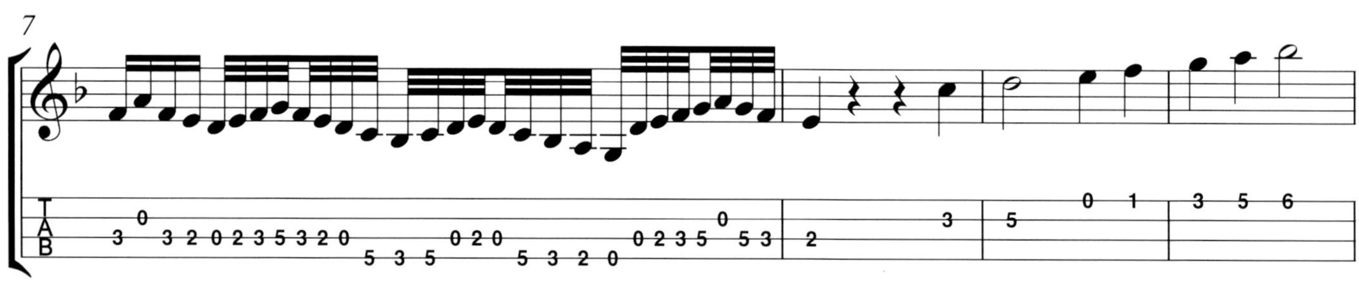


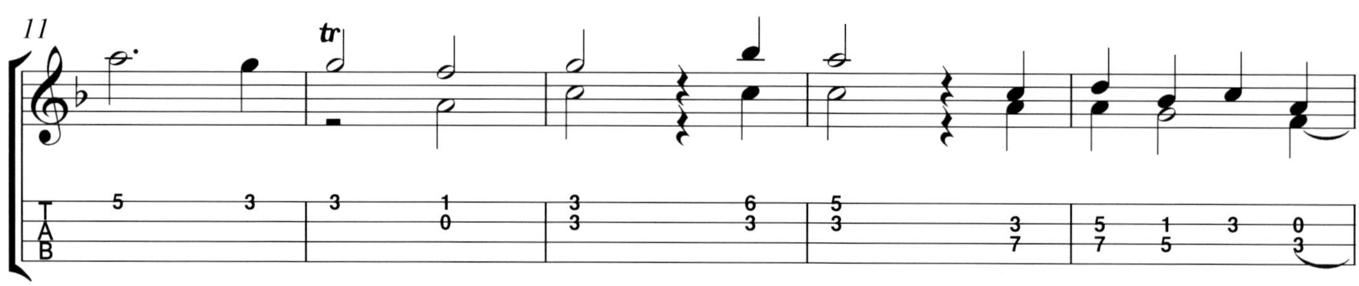

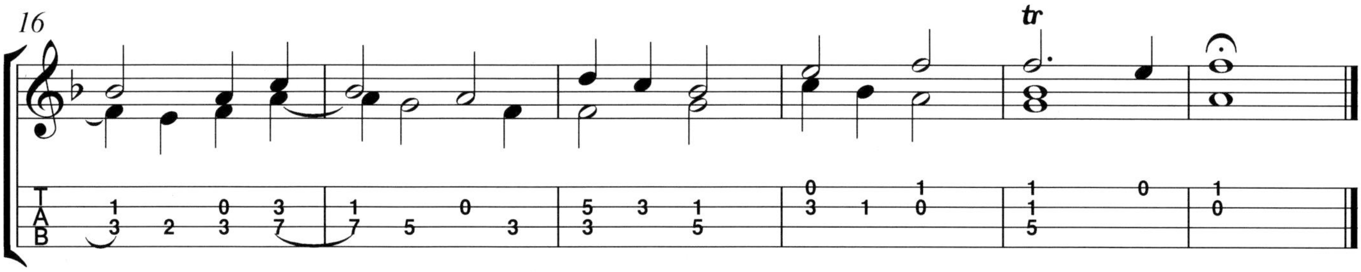


# Sonata VI

## Preludio

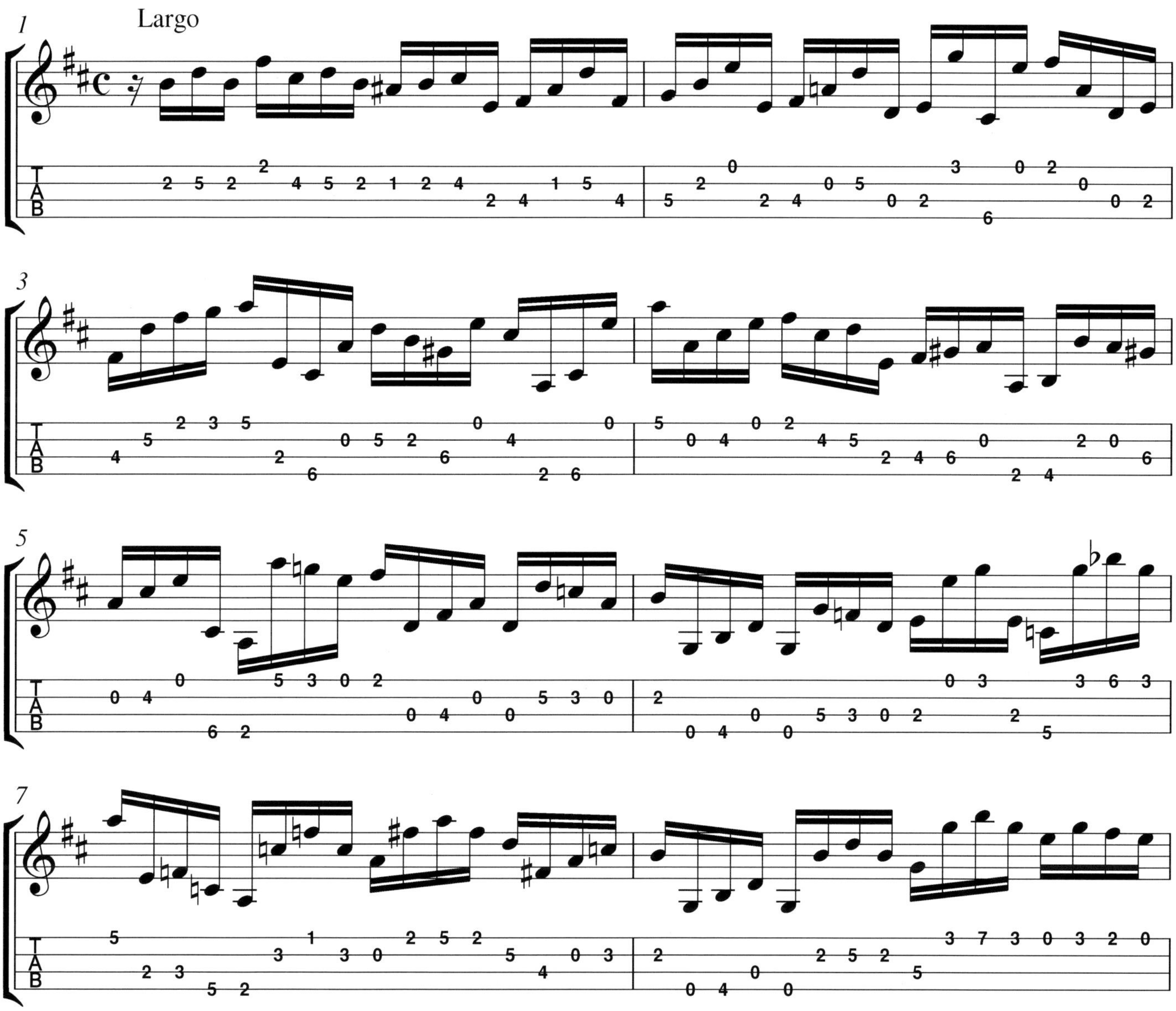

9
11
13
16
19
Adagio
24
Adagio

# Allemanda

11
16
tr
22
27
31
tr
T
A
B

# Corrente

# Sarabanda

# Giga

22
tr
25
28
30

# Finale

# Other Recommended Mandolin Books

J.S. Bach Mandolin Duets (Holenko)

100 Techniques & Exercises for Mandolinists (Mair)

Playford for Mandolin (Goodin)

Bach E Major Prelude from the Partita No. 3 Transcribed for Mandolin (Driscoll)

Baroque Music for Mandolin (Bancalari)

12 Divertimentos for Solo Mandolin by James Oswald (Goodin)

Italian Folk Music for Mandolin (LaBarbera)

J.S. Bach for Mandolin (Bancalari)

Renaissance Tunebook (Holenko)

Traditional Southern Italian Mandolin and Fiddle (LaBarbera)

Complete Mandolinist (Mair)

Northern Italian & Ticino Region Folk Songs for Mandolin (Aonzo, Ponzoni & Borsani)

Cantabile (Baldassari & Mock)

Bach's Sonatas and Partitas for Solo Violin Arranged by Mandolin (Driscoll)

Telemann for Mandolin (Goodin)

Romantic Melodies for Mandolin Solo (Landau)

Vivaldi Concertos for Mandolin (Lemma)

J.S. Bach: Two Part Inventions for Mandolin (Bancalari)

International Favorites for Mandolin (Carr)

13 Tango Passions for Mandolin and Guitar (Karasik)

Contra Dance Encyclopedia (Holenko)

Mandolin Classics (Cherednik and Eidson)

Mandolin Instrumentals (Landau)

Mandolin Scales and Studies (Bell)

Renaissance Solos for Mandolin (Holenko)

Mandolin Sampler (Gelo)

Mandolin Technique Studies (Raum)

Mandolin Classics in Tablature (Bancalari)

***WWW.MELBAY.COM***